John Ap Thomas Jones

The Retrospect

A Poem in Four Cantons

John Ap Thomas Jones

The Retrospect
A Poem in Four Cantons

ISBN/EAN: 9783744685214

Printed in Europe, USA, Canada, Australia, Japan

Cover: Foto ©Thomas Meinert / pixelio.de

More available books at **www.hansebooks.com**

"Westward the course of empire takes its way."—BERKELEY.

THE RETROSPECT.

A POEM.

IN FOUR CANTOS.

BY
JOHN AP THOMAS JONES.

PHILADELPHIA:
J. B. LIPPINCOTT & CO.
1884.

Copyright, 1884, by JOHN AP THOMAS JONES.

PREFACE.

In presenting "The Retrospect" to the public the author deems it almost unnecessary to follow the usual custom of an introductory explanation. The poem, *which must speak for itself*, had its origin simply in the recreation of leisure hours. But, the prompting of its inspiration is freely admitted as having a higher purpose; for often has the author felt an impassioned desire, as he saw the march of progress sweeping away every landmark of the pioneer and early emigrant, to rescue if possible from oblivion, not their historic record, but the memory of that spirit which controlled those days of our Arcadian simplicity. As a narrative poem the style adopted is that flowing, familiar measure easily read, and always popular: while the language aims to be forcible without ostentation, plain without commonplace. The experience of the writer has particularly qualified him for the work; as a familiar intercourse with many of those old characters, now passed away, has, through their lives and their traditions, given him a fund of information: while the landscapes depicted are but the developments of scenery impressed from nature upon his mind. So having finished his task, a pleasure within itself, he presents it to the public, for what it is worth, as the work of one who always loved the picturesque and poetic in the history of his people.

THE RETROSPECT.

CANTO I.

'Twas eve—the sun had grandly rolled,
Through crimson clouds all fringed with gold,
   In triumph down the west;
But left behind, as king of day,
His twilight's soft enchanting ray,
   To meditations blest.
A thousand plants, of Summer's bloom,
Were blending in one sweet perfume
   Their breath upon the air;
Where all, in bliss, appeared to fill
Life's transient cup without an ill,
   As once did Eden fair.
A stately mansion near us stood
Beneath a grand old grove of wood,

Whose ancient roots searched deep the ground,
Whose giant limbs on high around
Their leafy branches spread above,
Like wings that shield a brood of love.

This home, beneath this sylvan shade,
   Was of a taste refined;
Around its handsome colonnade
   The woodbine sweetly twined:
While on the lawn, refreshing, cool,
There stood a bass-carved marble pool;
   Where nymph-like fountains tossed their spray
In crystals o'er a sportive school
   Of golden fish at play.
From thence, we saw the distance bound
By chains of mountain foot-hills round;
   While in the valley lay
A spacious city sending high
Her towering steeples, to the sky,
   Which caught the coming ray

Of rising Cynthia, queen of night,
Whose silvery sheen, in ripples bright,
Danced on a river, rolling free
Through rosy banks, to greet the sea.

This landscape, though with beauty spread,
   Would be to me of little care;—
Earth's grandest scenes are cheerless—dead!
   If woman never enters there.
In Eden, e'en, when Time had birth,
   Who could its loneliness withstand?
But woman came!—the gem of earth,
   The masterpiece of nature's hand!
Then changed indeed!—how bright the hour!
   When radiant beauty spread around
Her charms; which paled the fairest flower
   That bloomed on man's celestial ground.

So on the active stage of strife
We'll raise the veil; displaying life
   In scenes that might regale

THE RETROSPECT.

The senses with adventures wild;
Or charm with love's devotions mild;
Like strange Aladdin's tale.

Grouped on the colonnade a band
Of lassies clustered in their prime,
Like fairies from a dreamer's land;
Or goddesses of Homer's time.
Their tresses,—some retained the ray
Of gold that crowned the parting day;
While some, their sable locks so bright,
Reflected back the coming night;—
And this bright group, all young and fair,
Sat building castles in the air.

An aged grandam sat alone,
The queen of life's domestic throne;
A link she seemed, by nature cast
In silver, with the buried past:
Her locks were bleached in sorrow's tide,
Fair as the robes that deck the bride;

THE RETROSPECT.

Yet stately was her mien and grace,
Though care had marked her noble face.

Her mind was calling in review
  The times of fourscore years or more;
Her dreams awoke old scenes anew
  That long had slept in mem'ry's store.
The stars were lighting up the sky;
  But she their beauty heeded not.
The fire-flies were flashing nigh;
  Yet things around were all forgot.
'Twas in the past her vision trod,
  Retracing all her paths of time;
Or paused, to view the verdant sod
  Where sleeps her own best love sublime.
It was a pensive hour to dwell
  On dreamy hopes, or fading past,
To thrill the soul with rapture's swell
  In visions far too bright to last.

'Twas then a lady with an air
Of matron grace, relieved from care,

Stepped forth, exclaiming with surprise,
As beaming nature met her eyes:
Oh, grandma! see! Oh, what a sight!
How grand the moon shines out to-night!
It looks—it seems the world awhile
Is bathed in nature's sweetest smile!
It was not always thus you've seen
This word in tranquil bliss serene:
I've told these girls how you could tell
Them many a changing story well;
For you are last of all our race
Who first had settled in this place.

The youthful band took up the plea,
While moving round like fairies free,
They pressed her hard, in merry glee,
   To hear her story told.
With zeal they gave her love's embrace,
They smoothed her brow, they kissed her face,
Until with unaffected grace
   She gave these tales as told.

THE RETROSPECT. 11

My children, I was dreaming how
   Old scenes have changed, for once the space
Below was one wild wood, but now
   A mighty city fills the place.
Great grandeur fell before the hand
That came to delve and till the land;
That laid the stately forest low,
To gain what labor might bestow.

Back, far as mem'ry bears my dreams
I see—or so to me it seems—
A village fair, of rural taste,
Its church refined, its mansions chaste;
And then a scene,—a busy scene,—
A moving long comes in between
   That place and after-years.
But I will make my theme to-night
The changes that occurred in sight;—
   Tales of the pioneers.

My father's bold and restless will
Was of a nature naught could still;

The settled scenes he left behind
Were fetters to his iron mind;
So like a royal bird that spread
Its wings for freedom, father fled,
Away from men! away he flew!
It mattered not!—he little knew!—
Until he found this place to fill
The measure of his reckless will.

When first we came no human sound
Had broke the solitude around,
Save but the savage of our race
Who prowled the wood in search of chase:
And I have seen the red man stand
   In rapt amazement to behold
Reared on his choicest hunting land
   The wigwam of the Paleface bold.

'Twas then indeed sublime to see
The untouched forests waving free;
These valleys, far as eye can reach,
With ash, the oak, the birch, the beech,

The walnut, elms,—were filled in fine
With trees unnumbered ; and the pine
Crowned like the plumes of royal pride
Each mountain-top; while down the side
The cypress and the cedar grew
In majesty, to charm the view.

That spot where stands yon marble dome,
   To all my youthful memories dear,
Was where my father built his home
   Of logs, felled in the forest near.
With loam and leaves he made it proof
   In every seam against the roar
Of winter's blast, and for the roof
   He spread with bark the structure o'er.
The chimney and the hearth he made
Of wicker-work, and overlaid
Them both within and out, entire,
With mud, to guard against the fire ;—
But all was strongly built for war :
The very planks that formed the door

Were riven from old oaken forms
Whose strength had braved a thousand storms.

On wings of thought I wander back
To childhood's days, o'er memory's track;—
I see them now—in every change
Of beauty and of terrors strange.
When nights were long and winters cold,
   The wolves would prowl in hunger near,—
Around the house,—while in the fold
   The frightened lambs all cringed with fear.
The bears, the panthers, and a score
Of consternations spread before
My youthful path, when yet a child
I ventured in the forest wild.
But violets sweet, and daisies bright,
And roses wild allured the sight,
And made me all forgetful roam
In realms of beauty round my home:
And madly, too, I loved the rills,
The ceaseless music of the hills,

Ere they their final leap would take,
To rest forever in the lake.
But oh, how changed!—those waters feel
Upon the lake the ploughing keel;—
Those dancing rills are led to trace
Their sluggish way along a race,
Until each bridled stream is made
To turn the grinding wheels of trade.

But we should not repine though gone,
Great nature's charm—for at the dawn
Of culture, came in beauty's stead,
Security instead of dread;
Security to live in peace;
  Security for honest toil;
Security for that increase
  Which wastes not as the huntsman's spoil.

Not long alone were we, for soon
Another came,—I think 'twas June?—
The second June, when all was bright!
A stranger paused before a sight

As fair to see as e'er the earth
Displayed since Mother Nature's birth.
The man was of colossal size ;
Strong as an oak ; with eagle eyes :
Quick as a panther, and as bold
A man as ever dared the wold.
The wife, in contrast by his side,
Unfit to stem life's stormy tide,
Was of a nature calm and mild ;
And she was God's anointed child.
One child had they,—but one,—and he
Was like his father strong and free,
While from his mother's soul he drew
The grace of God that made him true.

And this was Reuben,—bless the boy !
   Who through my days of childhood's play
Was my protector, guide, and joy,
   And in my after-years my stay.
Once, I remember well when we
   Went forth to greet the fragrant spring ;

THE RETROSPECT.

Went forth in youth, with spirits free,
    When song was on the feathered wing;
For all the grove seemed then alive
With birds, and bees, in nature's hive.
The birds sang love-songs in the bower;
The bees sipped honey from each flower;
While we went forth to hail with pride
The vernal charms on every side.
Yes,—we beneath those arbors green
    Of arching boughs in heedless play,
Went onward, charmed with every scene,
    Regardless where their paths would stray,—
Went onward, weaving garlands sweet,
Of buds and blossoms at our feet;
For he declared, from east to west
He'd cull the gems of Flora's best,
To twine a diadem for me;
The peerless queen of Flora's lea.

But soon beclouded was that dream;
For in a glen where scarce a beam

Of searching sunlight's strength could learn
The depth of that dark vale of fern,
We lost our way;—yes, lost our path,
As if the spirit, dark, of wrath,
In evil mood, had come to blight
That glow of transient blisses bright.

Lost! lost! I know that awful sound,
With solitude supreme around.
It checked my blood like winter's blast;
That moment seemed indeed my last;
For all in terror, where I stood,
I saw but danger's boundless wood.
But in his strength, of manly might,
He led me where a sunbeam bright
Broke through a glade; and as he smiled
He asked me, " Are you yet a child ?"
A child!—As I that question caught,
It raised a strange, o'erwhelming thought,
For I had sprung as girlhood grows,
A bud just blooming out a rose.

And oh! estranged!—there seemed to yawn
  Between me and my friend of old
A wondrous gulf, when reason's dawn
  Revealed myself of woman's mould.

Instinctively I shrank away,—
Doubt, fear, on that eventful day,
Possessed my soul, till Reuben's mind
Displayed itself in acts refined—
In self-reliant courage rare;
In gentle words, in tender care;
Until my feelings soon regained
That confidence his life sustained.
Bold was his step while leading on:
  Light as an antelope and free;
One well might deem all danger gone
  Who had the privilege to see.
But as I watched each anxious look
  With which his roving eye would stray,
I saw with every path he took
  'Twas hope alone that led the way.

THE RETROSPECT.

Then I to cheer him, o'er and o'er
Went prattling fancy's mystic lore,
To draw from superstition, hope
Found only in diviner scope:
For where religion fails to hold
A people in its sacred fold,
Their hungry souls are sure to cling
For comfort to some occult thing.
So in that wild, unsettled life
   The daring pioneer must lead,
He finds but little through the strife
   On which the Christian soul can feed.
The very nature of his mind
Has rent him from a world refined
And sent him, like a morning ray,
The herald of a coming day.
We had no caste distinctions there;
The learned, the coarse, the tender fair
Leaned all alike on common might,
For safety, in a savage fright.
And superstition's idle dream
Held almost every hope supreme:

They pow-wowed o'er their sick for health;
Misfortunes came by witches' stealth,
And great were they whose charm could break
The coil of the wizard's snake.

One wild old waif surpassed them all;
 Her land, her lineage, none could tell;
O'er spirits great, or spirits small,
 She claimed to hold a magic spell.
Half savage, and half civilized,
Old Cora seemed, and highly prized
The faith, the honor, and the dread
Her very presence round her spread.
A captive maiden, crushed, a slave
Her lot had been to serve her brave;
Till hardship ploughed each gentle trace
Of woman from her wrinkled face;—
Then, like a sibyl-crone of old,
She gained a power uncontrolled
O'er Indian,—and the white as well!
For none disputed Cora's spell.

Her tales were those I told that day,
To cheer us on our doubtful way.
Tales of the Fairy Spirits bright,
Born, as she said, of air and light;
When Spring returns with all her cheer,
The mother of the fruitful year.
These tiny elves seemed in her mind
To hold a spirit place refined;
Created for the special good
Of guarding mortals in the wood.

I've heard her tell with zealous vim,
Tell how they came in fairy-trim;
Tell how the snow-drop, blooming white,
Was planted first by their Frigid Knight
As he came in furs,—to prepare the way
  For the King and Queen,
  In their beautiful sheen,
At the head of their grand array.
And how the Queen, on her butterfly,
Rode with her maids of honor nigh;

While the monarch bold,
On his bug of gold,
Led his host with banners high;—
With flaunting banners! but instead of drum,
The music he brought was the wild-bees' hum,
Who fed, from their bags of honey-dew,
The motley throng of the Fairy crew.

And the rank and file would gather, she said,
Gather by night, in a moonlit glade;
In mirth and might, yet ceased their sport
To build a throne for their royal court;—
All built of th' soft white silver-light
That falls from the moon on a Fairy-night.

But the beautiful Queen was the brilliant theme
That roused the crone to her brightest dream.
Clad, as she said, in gossamer blue,
That changed and turned to every hue
The Fairies from the rainbow drew,
Or robbed from every flower.

And the crown she wore was a golden stream
The Fairies plucked from a morning beam;
Twined and twisted, with many a gem
Of rosy-dew, in a diadem
   That glistened through the bower:
Where all supreme she ruled in might;
While forth her King, with armies bright,
Sped out to guard their wood by night;
   In pomp of Fairy power.

Here Cora's face would darkly scowl,
Her voice assume a sullen growl,
As she described old Giant Grim;
His bulky form, his massive limb,
His staff made of a lofty tree
With which he strode the forest free,
Or stalked across the hills, to steal
A brace of mortals for his meal.

Then bright her wrinkled features grew,
As wild her zeal and fancy drew

The fall of Giant Grim.
'Twas on a night, the moon shone bright,
The Fairy choir, by its light,
　　Had sung their evening hymn;
When all were startled by the sound
Of screams; and by the trembling ground,
That told the Giant prowled around,
　　With mortals in his hand.
Then to her herald-cricket gave
The Queen command, to call the brave
Around the trysting-tree, to save
　　That earth-born helpless band.

The Fairies hearing, left their mirth
In swarms, from trees, and caves of earth;
They left, from where the blooming rose
Concealed the butterfly's repose;
And from the ferns, where waters leap
Along the rock-bound chasm deep,
To do their Royal King's command;
As guards of their enchanted land.

And as her tale went on to say,
The King arrived in armed array;
Where, mounting on his toadstool-stand,
He hailed his legions of command;
And made in hurried accent loud
This proclamation to the crowd:
"Ye Braves! we have a word to say,—
Stands here a single knightly fay
Who lance in hand, amid this gloom,
Will save these mortals from their doom?
If so!—we pledge our Crown and Life,
Our Royal Child shall be his wife!"

Forth stepped a knightly fay of fame,
She said 'twas Fairy Dare, by name;
His tiny form, right brave to see,
Was armed a soldier cap-a-pie.
His helmet was a skull, bleached white,
Of humming-bird gained in a fight;
The plates that formed his coat of mail
Were gold and silver; each a scale

Of tiny fish, wrecked on the strand
Where surging oceans storm the land.

" My Liege," the little knight replied,
" One word before I leave your side ;—
My lance unbought is for the right ;—
At your command I charge to-night :
And if I die, let no one say
I died a mercenary Fay,
Or that I failed my King's command,
Till purchased by his daughter's hand ;
If I return—I now disown
All claims ;—unless from her alone."

Then to the air he spread his wings,
Two gauze-like, gilded, speckled things,
And like in size but as a fly,
Dare perched on Grim's great shoulder high,
Where long he held his thorny lance,
Awaiting but a Fairy's chance
   To work his purpose well.

He climbed the hair and eyelids near;
Explored within the Giant's ear;
But not a vital spot he found
In all his explorations round,
  Till in a weary spell
The Giant sought refreshing sleep;
Beneath a thicket dark and deep,
  Where scarce a moon-beam fell.

Then for his work the Fay prepared,
  When searching round he found, forsooth!
A chance that desperation dared,
  A cavern in a hollow tooth.
So, in the tooth without reserve
  The Fairy hid, to try his game,
Of battling on the laughing nerve;—
  The nerve that ruled the Giant's frame.

I cannot now, at this late date,
Do justice to, or half relate
Old Cora's story of that strife
The Fairy waged for human life.

But from his cave, all undeterred,
The Giant's tongue with might he speared,
Until the wood and hills around
Were moved by one unearthly sound
Of laughter loud ;—that scarce a bird
Has since that night in song been heard ;
Except the owl, who in dismay
Screams frightful yet for dawning day.

But Dare he tickled, might and main ;
He scratched, he thrust, he charged again ;
While Grim with howling laughter rolled,
For laughter all his force controlled,
Until he weak, and weaker grew,
As he in fierce contortions threw
Himself around, and gasped for breath,
Till Dare had tickled him to death.

Then Cora told in mirthful glee
How merry Dare leaped forth to see
The helpless mortals safe and free ;

And how he blew his tiny horn;
And how the signal back was borne,
That called the Fay of phantom light
With all his Jack-a-lanterns bright;
Who lured the lost bewildered through
The wood to homeward paths they knew.

These tales, and more, I told that day,
A parrot keeping fear at bay;
And I in faith, indeed, believed
Those tales, as truths by most received.
But looking up, I saw revealed
In Reuben's smile a doubt concealed,
That banished every hope I drew
Of help from Cora's Fairy crew.

Oh! I remember every trace
Of Reuben's frank, expressive face,
As I besought him thus to tell
What he believed of spirits fell.—
I told him, father said a youth
    He was of deep discernment keen;

And begged him, O, to tell in truth
If he had e'er a fairy seen?
For I have heard grim stories old,
I said, of ghosts and giants dread;
Until my very blood ran cold,
And terror dazed my reeling head.
But you are always calm and still;
You seem to fear no earthly sound;
What is it that controls your will?
Are there no terrors lurking round?
I've often dwelt in quiet dream
How grand it is to be like you;
And longed to drink that precious stream,
Which makes a life so brave and true.

" I never saw," he said, " nor could,
These air-born spirits of the wood.
They spring from superstition's brain,
Or from the poet's dreamy strain,
To terrify, or please the mind,
Of ignorance, or taste refined.

But one I know, of passing worth,
A fairy form-like child of earth,
Who far excels in beauty rare
Your figment spirits of the air.
'Tis not her robes of gaudy glow
Plucked from the storm-cloud's brilliant bow,
But sparkling eyes dark as the night,
A heart supreme in all that's right;"—

But modesty forbids me tell
His glowing words of praise, that fell,
Like sounds eolian, on my ear,
And thrilled me with a love sincere.
I answered not. I could not speak.
I felt the crimson in my cheek:
But with an impulse naught could check
I threw my arms around his neck;
For in my breast had burst the same
Bright glow that rose from Eden's flame,
When God first gave to man in bliss
The rapture of Eve's loving kiss.

THE RETROSPECT. 33

True love is life's celestial flame,
    A lamp that lights earth's darkest hour,—
It was a bridal-gift that came
    When man, a new created power,
Walked in the rich ambrosial grove
    Of Eden, ere he fell from grace:
'Twas God his Maker gave him love,
    Before he lost that sacred place.
It was the only gift divine
    He bore from thence. It never dies!—
'Tis Heaven's own!—and yet 'tis mine!
    To bless the earth! and bless the skies!
O, sacred thought! I wait the store
    When I shall join my friends above,
Where we shall meet, to part no more,
    Around the hallow'd throne of love!

That day, on rapture's pinions bright,
Care took an eagle's airy flight
Awhile away; till terror's dread
Aroused us to those dangers spread

Around us there,—and changed the dream
Of earth to hope's almighty theme.
He cheered me on with tales of love,—
Celestial love,—how God above
Beholds our wants, and sends us aid
Unseen, in every form :—he said,
" God sends us blessings in each shower ;
He breathes from every perfume-flower ;
He whispers in the rippling rills ;
He made the everlasting hills ;
And do you think He would forget
A soul on which His seal is set ?—
That seal that binds us to His shrine
Of hope eternal ; all divine !"

Then smilingly, he said, " And you
Have wondered whence the stream I drew,
Those waters that have made me hail
With coldness every idle tale,
That fills this grand majestic place
With people of a goblin race.

" Know then, that stream the saints revered ;
'Tis inspiration's Holy Word :
Through every page salvation flows ;
There, Glory's crown of mercy glows ;
And there alone can sorrow find
The balm that heals the wounded mind."
I then knew little of that Book,
For hope-eternal's shining brook
Had scarcely cast its flaky foam
Around my good, but worldly home.

But Reuben's soul was like a star
Lit from the shining gates, ajar,
And cast that day its light o'er me ;
A light that set my spirit free.
He first described in flights superb
The beauty of the Sacred Word ;
How by the voice of God divine
The sun and stars were bid to shine ;
And how the cloud of glory rolled
Through Zion's temple, lined with gold ;

And closed, at last, where John relates
His visions of the pearly gates.

And then he spoke of Giant Grim ;—
Of Satan's power ;—and told of him
Who prowled, and prowls the stricken earth
In fury since creation's birth.
How by ambition's fault he fell,
An angel peer, to rule in hell ;
And how he wears a subtle smile,
The thoughtless worldlings to beguile,
As raving through the earth he strolls :—
The ruin of immortal souls !

But when he touched that theme above
All other themes,—the theme of love,
His mind ! his soul ! his spirit fired !
He spoke ! he looked ! like one inspired.
And in my mind I saw the view
Of Jesus crucified he drew.

I saw the crown of plaited thorn;
The sacred brow of mercy torn;
The crimson drops of hallow'd blood,
Each drop a world's redemptive flood.
I saw the anguish of the eye;—
I heard the Mediator cry;—
While from the cross appeared to shine
Refulgent beams of light divine.—
That day—its mem'ries sweet remain;
For I, that day, was born again!—
Born in a wilderness untrod
By Christian foot, a child of God!

Born of the Spirit!—Thought sublime!—
  O, who unmoved can on it dwell?
A life that knows no roll of time!—
  A holy gift!—a hallow'd spell!—
A person of the Triune one,—
The Comforter sent by the Son;
We scarcely dream a Godhead form
Keeps every Christ-born spirit warm.

To mortal minds His hallow'd course
Seems often but a subtle force,
Like dews that fall upon the earth,
To feed the things of soulless birth.
Yet strange!—to some He comes with power,
As lightning through a summer shower;
To strike the proud—the haughty down;
Like rocks rent from the mountain's crown.
While some, in grace, grow like the gem
Of vernal life, on nature's stem,—
A doubtful speck that's scarcely seen,—
A larger bulb of leafy green,—
A bursting bud,—a brilliant bloom,
That fills the air with sweet perfume.

I've seen myself a man of sin
Touched by a monitor within;
Who trembled like the aspen leaf
When first he heard, with bitter grief,
The lost estate of those who scorn
The blessings of the sacred born.

I saw him bowed in anxious prayer,—
I heard him cry in wild despair;
When to his soul the Spirit came
And filled with light that child of shame.
His form changed not;—his rough, scarred face
Lost not a single earthly trace;
But when he spoke—profaneless,—calm;
We found the wolf was born a lamb.
That man to sin was shackled fast,
Till Jesus cleansed him from the past.

But to my tale: The sun for rest
Was fast descending in the west,
When, wearied, near a gnarled old oak,
We tarried by a spring that broke,
As if to cheer our dark despair,
Bright from a rock, in crystals clear.
We bathed our faces,—drink refreshed
Our anxious hopes, by fear oppressed;
When turning round I asked him there,
To plead of God a guide in prayer.

Grand was that orison he made,
That God would guide us from that glade;
It sparkled, like the dewy leaf,
With sacred faith and firm belief;
And poured in love's most earnest plea,
It seemed a prayer alone for me.

The prayer was done. The quiet hush
Was broken by a rustling bush,
That startled both with sudden doubt,
When father's dog sprang wildly out;
And dancing, leaping from the ground,
As if he felt the lost were found,
Went circling round, and ran before,
A guide to my own father's door.
That day was one with danger fraught.
That day was one of sacred thought:
Yet blest is still to me that day
I learned to love, and learned to pray.

CANTO II.

THE great-grandmother paused, for here
   Her story reached its seeming close;
Amid those scenes, to memory dear,
   Where hope had found repose.
Amid those scenes, while years remain,
The aged love to walk again;
Transported o'er a world of care
To youth's Elysian fields of air.
But those around, with youthful praise,
Besought her to recount her days
That followed those in that wild grove;
And tell the sequel of her love.
But she, the ancient, dwelt in thought
Like one by seeming doubts o'erwrought,
Until her eye revealed the span
Of doubt was past; and thus began :

No dream of words can ever paint
    Devotion fond,—sublimely true:
Love-pictures are but shadows faint
    The poet's genius spreads to view.
True hearts, like crystal drops that meet
    Upon the petal of a flower,
Are blended in one union sweet;
    Defying fancy's brightest power.
Love smooths the troubled path of life;
    For, like the calm and limpid tide,
It flows above the ills of strife;
    As waters o'er the rocks they hide.
And so the world rolled smoothly on,
    Nor marked we how the years swept by,
As time entwined our souls as one,
    In love, in hope, in rapture's tie.

The seasons changed,—enchanting flew,
    Without a change between us two;
Although, by observation, they
    Are often types of love's display.

THE RETROSPECT.

We see the south winds softly bring
Coquettish promise in the spring;
Then turn and fly with all their charms,
And leave the world in winter's arms.
So oft the doubtful lovers fly;—
A yearning youth,—a maiden shy,—
When but devotion's earnest sigh
Would melt the frost of folly's fear,
And bid the bloom of hope appear.
All bliss was ours. A buoyant time
Swept over Reuben's spring, and mine:
No storms disturbed our peaceful rest,
No icy doubt chilled either breast.
For us sweet Flora, through the bowers,
Strewed nothing but her choicest flowers.

Then tranquil summer—bright in June—
   Comes with her ripening rays above,—
Comes with the mocking-bird's sweet tune,—
   Comes with her brilliant beams of love
     That strengthen day by day;

Until the swain, where labor spread
The seed of faith, beholds his bread
    In harvest's rich array.
So love's implanted faith sublime
Grows stronger 'neath the roll of time,
Like to that blazing orb on high,
Undimmed, undying in the sky.
All brilliant were our summers,—we
Were rustics then—both strong and free,
    Who gathered in the field
With all the neighbors round,—for hands
Were few in those fresh broken lands,—
    To harvest in the yield.
And merry were those days, when all
Each other helped, both great and small,
And swelled at noon the chorus long,
That lengthened out the harvest song.
Where Reuben reaped, I followed there,
To bind with skill, and loving care,
Our golden sheaves, and have them stand
The praise and pride of all the band.

Then when at eve the twilight's ray
Dispersed the laborers of the day,
We homeward strolled, while all was still,
Save but, perhaps, the whip-poor-will,
And talked love's air-built castles o'er :
The garners of youth's hopeful store.

Then Autumn, in her gaudy pride,
   A transformation comes,—a show
Of beauty, as the forest wide
   Displays its changing leaves aglow ;
Like love's life-sunset when the twain
Have reached their autumn, sans a stain.
In their kaleidoscope of years,
Unblighted by remorseful tears,
They see revolving o'er and o'er
Their brightly-tinted days of yore ;
Or see around the ripened fruit,
Of children trained without dispute ;
Where aged, honored, parents blest
May pillow on affection's 'reast —

But discord sows a bitter seed;
When age shall feel devotion's need,
Alone, they'll find, though sorrow grieves,
But Autumn's dry, dead, cheerless leaves.
The seasons changed, the seasons flew,
Without a change between us two.
Our love was like the pine as seen;
It lived in strength a fadeless green
Through summer's suns, and winter's roar,
Till time to Reuben was no more.

E'en when the howling Winter came
With sleeting storms and driving rain,
It still had pleasures in its flow;
Though earth was shrouded o'er with snow.
For brighter than the sparkling lights
Of jewel stars, on frosty nights,
Are lovers' hopes; when round the blaze
They talk, and dream, of brighter days.

I often stop to ponder how
The things have changed 'tween then and now:

THE RETROSPECT.

This house so grand, with comforts rare,
Its frescoed walls, and finished stair,
Its velvet floors, and stately dome,
And wonder can it be my home.
And strange it seems from far below
The furnace sends its pleasant glow
Of heat so mild, through every room,
That melts away the winter's gloom;
As if the art of man could bring
The fairy breeze of endless spring.

And when I wander through yon mill
The sight around seems stranger still;
The spinning-mule's unnumbered reels
Have far eclipsed the rustic wheels,
And cast a blessing o'er the land,
Where once the overburdened hand
Of woman, night and day to win
But comforts small, would toil and spin;
To spin and toil she seemed a slave,
Between the cradle and the grave.

Yet all these modern things of art
May be but trammels on the heart;
That throbs in forest homes as free
As boughs wave on the mountain tree.

Our cabin home,—I know it well.
No royal palace can excel,
In charming bliss, the winter night,
When hearts were warm and sorrows light;
As we sat 'round the blazing hearth
All buoyant love, all simple mirth,
To tell the ventures of the day,
Or watch the young at rustic play.
And when I hear the modern strain
It wafts me to that home again;
And in my heart I keenly feel
The music of the spinning-wheel,
When I would sit with Reuben nigh
And spin the flax, that seemed to tie
Our hearts, our hopes, our thoughts as one,
With every thread my fingers spun.

But many a day's auspicious morn
Has been ere noon all tempest torn ;—
Yes, many a ship of royal power
Has foundered in its proudest hour!—
Once, when the broad green woodlands round
Seemed wrapped in lasting peace profound,
A band of wealthy strangers came,
As huntsmen searching after game.
A guide they sought around our place,
One skilled ;—who knew the wary chase ;
And pressed my Reuben, whom they made
Their leader, through the woodland-glade ;—
For he was formed by nature's hand,
A man majestic, to command!

There was among that stranger train
A popinjay,—of follies vain ;
Who pleaded sickness,—want of care ;—
A nurse among the ladies fair ;
And stayed behind, to play the part
Of foolish suitor for my heart.

He told me tales of foreign climes;
He changed his theme to rapture's rhymes;
He spoke of mansions rich and grand;
And placed them all at my command.
But O! the contrast grandly shed
A halo round my Reuben's head;—
That weakling, to my darling one,
Was as a rush-light to the sun.

Three fleeting days had scarcely passed
   Since Reuben forth the hunters led
Before our homes were overcast
   With deep solicitude and dread:
For near the spring, we found around
Deep Indian footprints o'er the ground;
Revealing death, and savage war,
In ambush near each scattered door.
Then darkly deep spread terror's shade,
For out preparing in the glade
The men, or nearly all, had gone
As trappers for the season long.

But Reuben and my father strove
To fortify there in the grove
Our home, the strongest and the best
Built on the frontier of the west.
And there the scattered people came,
The young, the old, the weak, the lame;
But when the men were counted o'er,
The stranger only numbered four.

. That day of days! that awful day!
The trembling crowd, with anxious flush,
Watched every movement of each bush;
For every bush, to all the crowd,
Was but grim Death's dark lurking shroud;—
The wolves we kept at bay!
Till day had measured out its span,
Then oh! Death's carnival began!—
That night! O night! that horrid night!
Oh, could but mercy quench that sight!
For when I see the leaping flame
The horrid vision turns my brain!—

Each Indian brought his fagot store,
By stealth, and placed them near the door;
Then with a fiend's malignant ire
They lit that pile of dreadful fire;—
The smothered smoke soon told the tale,
How naught but daring could avail;
The strong the weak sought to inspire
With hope, as higher rolled the fire;
While all the hordes of open hell
It seemed, had joined the war-whoop yell.

Despair then nerved those arms of oak;
But few and hurried words were spoke;
When wide the door was open flung!
And quick to death! and danger sprung!
Bold, noble hearts, who sold their lives
To save their children and their wives.—
But courage there could not avail;
For I, of all that peopled dale,
    Was left alone to tell
How by the blazing glare of light
They stood unequal in the fight;

And how, at bay, each daring brave,
Without the power to strike or save,
 By savage marksman fell.

Then, oh, the scene! the scene I saw!
No tiger ever licked his claw
For blood that from his victim flew
With half the zest those Indians drew
Of transport dark, while gloating o'er
Our writhing children's reeking gore!
But from the house, when wrapped in flame,
The last of all, the stranger came;
Not like a man, but raving wild,
He prayed for mercy like a child.
I swooned,—
 And when that night again
I saw through my bewildered brain,
The scene was changed,—in that dark hour
It looked to me like Pluto's bower.
I saw a fire,—a savage band,
In groups around a victim stand.

I saw the stranger, tightly bound,
In torture writhing on the ground.
I heard his wild, his piercing cries;
I saw them sear his gleaming eyes;
Then with a fiendish impulse dire,
They cast him on their smouldering fire;
And danced the war-dance, in their pride,
Until their helpless victim died.

Then stirring up their fire, till late,
They wrangled o'er my trembling fate;
When near a hideous Indian came,
A savage chief of bloody fame,
Who claimed, in English, that my life
He saved to be his pale-face wife.
Just then I saw the rifles' flash.
I screamed to hear their welcome crash.
Each friend had marked his savage well;
For every flash an Indian fell.
Surprise, and consternation dread,
Dispersed the rest; all quickly fled,

Except the one that sought my charms;—
He grasped me in his brawny arms,
And strove to make my form his shield,
While backing, sullen, from the field.

But one there was among that train
Who never drew his mark in vain;
I saw his face reflect the light,
As I have seen the moon by night
Reflect its cheering beams aglow
O'er hope's despairing paths below.
His shot was well reserved, to see
How best it might be used for me,
Then with a nerve-controlling will
He raised his rifle, calmly, still,—
But I was made so close a screen
The Indian's form was scarcely seen :—
At last his head showed but a trace,—
A flash !—his brain besmeared my face;
And I could draw sweet freedom's breath,
Though folded in the arms of death !

The hunters came,—but ah! too late!
Too late to change the doom of fate!
They found but death around the place
Where all was life before the chase.
Then hard upon the savage trail
They pressed, to see what might avail,
But failed to reach the camp before
The tophet-dance of death was o'er.
As Reuben reconnoitred round
He saw me pinioned, on the ground,
Then gave in haste his hurried plan,
How every one should mark his man;—
That he alone would save me, there,
Or perish in that savage lair.
The work was done;—but oh, the sorrow!
His all were gone,—but me—his Laura;
And as I stood there breathing free,
He was the all fate left to me.

I soon became my Reuben's bride;—
Both one in love, naught could divide,
Till death removed him from my side,

THE RETROSPECT.

    And left me years ago
Alone in this cold world, to wait
Till we shall meet within that gate
Where Christ receives his own in state;—
    The ransomed from below.

The smoke that rose that tragic night
Rolled o'er and filled the land with fright,
As when the Lord's avenger swept
Through Egypt's skies, while Egypt wept
Beneath those dripping wings of dread,
That left in every home its dead.
The frontiers mustered in their fright;
The nation marched in martial might;
The drum, the fife, the trumpet's sound
Through days and nights re-echoed round;
And told the tale, how savage war
Had roused the land from shore to shore.

My Reuben, like a star of fate,
Rose o'er the tumult grand and great;

His light became the guide of all
Who gathered at the nation's call:
And rapid as the meteors fly,
His brilliant course swept upward, high;
Until he held supreme command
Of all the forces of this lan '.
His very presence seemed to fill
The soldiers with a dauntless will;
While with a corresponding fear
The savage held his presence near;—
For some believed the spirit Death
Obeyed the white chief's flaming breath.

The war rolled on with fearful force;
Destruction widely strewed its course
With tattered wigwams, scattered graves,
Green couches of unnumbered braves,
Who fell believing valor's hand
Could purge the white man from their land.
But Reuben's soul was bowed in grief,
To see them fall,—as falls the leaf,

And perish where they fell :
He sent to every tribe that bore
Their totem in that cruel war,
And bade them each their bravest send,
To meet in council, friend with friend,
In kindly greeting well.

Time passed,—but yet, at last they came;
Dark, sullen chiefs, of horrid fame,
In all their war-paint's fierce display,
In blankets robed,—in plumed array;
With arrows, tomahawks, and knives,
And scalps displayed, that told the lives
Each dastard slew ;—and how he tore
The vanquished victims of the war.

Arrangements then and there were made
To hold this council in the glade,
Where all was settled, as discreet,
That Indians and the whites should meet

Unarmed, except each leader grand,
Who came arrayed as in command.
 I saw that council;—'twas at night;
Within the centre, glowing rose
A fire that cast o'er friends and foes
 A weird-like phantom light.
The Indians round, upon the ground,
Appeared like ogres; not a sound
Fell from their lips; while those who came
For us, commissioners of fame,
Seemed moved by every fleeting change,
Of novelties around them strange.

At last the General—Reuben—rose,
Eyed by his fierce, relentless foes,
And thus addressed, in mercy's strain,
Why peace should bless the land again:

" Ye braves! to-night around this fire
We welcome every Indian sire!

THE RETROSPECT. 61

We meet you here to stay this wrong
That has accursed the land so long!
No woman's spirit nerves the whites
When striking for their home, and rights!
And well we know, a truth sincere,
An Indian never knew a fear!
But much we grieve to see the hands
Of soldiers armed, with swords and brands!
To see for naught your heroes die!
To hear your helpless orphans cry!
And now we pause to ask you why!—
Why shall we spread in death's array
Your braves as food for birds of prey?
Why shall they not live, love, and roam
In peace these forest glades their home?
Ye love your homes!—ye do them wrong
To battle with my people strong!
They would not strike if you would give
Them friendship for their love, and live
In peace and faith like brothers should,
That dwell together in the wood!

The same Great Spirit made us both!
The same Great Father marks the growth,
Of all his children!—why shall we
Contend against a fixed decree?
Why shall we not this slaughter cease?
And why not smoke the pipe of peace?
Why bury not the hatchet here,
In honor, faith, in love sincere,
And live beneath those laws that shed
Their peaceful blessings o'er each head?"

Then all was quiet; not a breath
Seemed moving o'er a scene of death,
When like the rustling of the leaves
The great Plausawa, chief of chiefs,
Arose, and I remember well
That man who seemed an evil spell.
His form was over middle height;
Compact, elastic, quick, and light;
His features like a vulture's beak;
An eagle-eye that well could seek

An unprotected place away,
Where he could swoop, and sweep his prey.
His face was painted red and blue;
Around his graceful form he threw
A panther-skin;—a royal gear,
Of eagle plumes and beaver-fur,
Adorned his head;—while, girt, he wore
His deadly weapons used in war.
And there this man, of fortune ill,
Arose and thus expressed his will:

"Brave Sungernumby,* hear ye me!—
The Spirit Great but smiles when he
Beholds his red men roving free!—
Yes, roving in these woodlands deep
He gave his forest-sons to keep!
Then why shall we that race admire
Who brought his people liquid fire?†
Who came with lightning‡ in their hand!

---

* Very strong man.•   † Whiskey.   ‡ Fire-arms.

Who came to desolate the land!
Whose love is in their blazing brand!
A race before whose blighting tread
Our food, the forest game, has fled.
Brave Sungernumby! you behold
In me the chieftain of this wold;—
You know me well!—for I command
The tribes around on every hand,
And in their name I tell you plain,
This land must yet be theirs again!
Two men once met when in the sky
The eye of day was rolling high;
The first, four moons, had wandered forth,
The howling spirit of the north:
His hair and beard of frosty white
Fell round a form of brawny might;
And he all homage would command,
As frost-chief of the frozen land.
The younger one, of blushing mould,
Who met this hoary figure cold,

THE RETROSPECT.

Wore on his head a wreath of flowers,
The happy child of blooming bowers;
Around whose spirit-form did cling
All fruitful blossoms, born of spring.
They met, these men, and built a blaze,
To talk to each of other days;
But as the first his story told
The second felt a blighting cold
Around his heart; and in despair
He almost fell a victim there.
The spirit white, by power strong,
Claimed all must by that right belong
To him!—for I can check the way,
He said, and mine shall be the sway!
If I a river meet,—but thrice
I blow my breath, when on the ice
I cross the stream, and 'neath my feet
The ground becomes a frozen sleet;
And all must yield where'er I go,
I bind with ice, and shroud with snow!

The ruddy Spirit-of-the-Spring
Smiled as he heard the braggart fling
A challenge out, for life or death,
Then calmly blew his perfumed breath,
When down he saw on either side
The boaster's arms in currents glide,
Who passed as mountain-mist away;
While Spring remained in full array.
Your words are smooth, great mighty chief,
But words can never give relief
When Indian children cry for bread!—
And can an Indian lay his head
In peace upon his land of shame,
From whence the Pale-face drove the game
And left him naught, but like a squaw,
To live beneath the white man's law?
Your words are strong, but while we blow
The breath of war your blood shall flow!
Like water!—till we drive you home!
Back—from these forests where we roam!"

"I'm sorry," Reuben then replied,
" To hear Plausawa now decide
To struggle on, in useless strife;
To waste away the red man's life.
My people, like the drops of rain,
Are numberless, o'er hill and plain!
And like the flood's resistless power
When thunders roll! and torrents shower!
They surging come!—and naught below
Can stay that freshet's onward flow!
Pause! pause, ye braves!—and think before
You give your counsel still for war!
Pause ere you send Death in his wrath,
To scorch, like lightning, every path!—
The white man would not strike you down;—
You need not live beneath his frown;—
We speak for peace, that all may rove
Like brothers through this mighty grove!
Remember how the whirlwinds sweep
The forests from the lofty steep!
So will the war sweep hill and plain
If we unbind its force again!

But if we bid these sorrows cease;
If we but pass the pipe of peace;
Its smoke will like the rainbow's cast,
Rejoicing tell the storm has passed.
We offer peace,—that it may cheer
The mother's hope—the children's fear;
And turn the heart of every brave
Toward his home, and not his grave.
Let every warrior pause and think!
For now ye stand upon the brink
Where but a step!—you may too late
Forever seal your nation's fate!—
These brothers great, who gather near,
Have come to see!—to talk!—and hear
From every brave—that burning grief,
For which by war he seeks relief!"

Then came a pause, long and profound,
Each heart beat its own muffled sound;
   But none their hope betrayed.

It seemed the angel dark of death
Was hov'ring o'er, and filled the breath
  Of every savage with despair,
    As they the time delayed.
  They saw unmoved Plausawa's air,
As he arose and sternly said,
  " My answer, braves, is but this knife!"
Then raised aloft his scalping blade,
  That terror of my life.
The Indians all on ruin bent
Responded,—grunting their assent;
When Reuben rose,—but no reply,—
  He calmly drew his shining sword,
Then scanning round, he raised it high,
  Accepting war without a word.

Fierce, wild, and dread, the struggle rolled;
O'er mountains,—plains,—when uncontrolled
Contention lit again the brand;—
Extermination stalked the land;
When armed for death was every hand,

Until Plausawa sank beneath
The war-cloud, on his wasted heath.

From that time on, whene'er I dwell
Upon the past, it seems a spell
Has wrought the wondrous changes wide
I see around on every side.
Below, a fort once held the ground,
    From whence we hear, like swarming bees,
The hum of yon great city's round
    Arising high on every breeze;
That tells how peace now bids them drive
Their business in that busy hive.

Yes, on a field of blood it grew,
This city—for the conflict drew
The men of every clime and cast
Together in the distant past.
There followed, first, the martial train,
A motley throng, for good or gain;

Like cormorants some, to seek th' yield,
As vultures seek the battle-field :—
To pluck the savage of his right;
To rob the soldier of his mite;
By every means to gather in
The price of sorrow, shame, or sin.

The honest trader;—and a crowd
Of restless spirits, true and proud,
Of stirring men, impulsive, strong,
At home alone in hurry's throng;—
And those who must excitement drink;
Although it dripped from terror's brink.

And then, again, the blessed few;
Moved only by kind feelings true.
Samaritans, who sought to bind
The cruel wounds war left behind.
They came commissioned from above,
Guides to the land of hallow'd love.

Where wars, and wounds, afflict no more
The ransomed on that deathless shore.

The conflict o'er,—the varied scope
Of every soldier found its hope,
Some, who had longed to reach the dome
Of peace parental, wandered home;
While many laid their armor down
And stopped, to build the growing town.

Crude was the hamlet first indeed
That rose to serve the moment's need,
Of shanties, huts, and cabins small;
The rover's lodge, the trader's stall;
Of boards, and logs, in rough array,
Built only for the pressing day.
But as the land filled up around,
As fields of culture clothed the ground,
The hamlet to a village grew;
For trade toward this centre drew:

And as the village gained renown
The place became a trading town.

I saw in all that social flow,—
That great commingling tide below,—
How man, with man, when left alone,
Was to his reckless nature prone.
But woman came, and like the dew
    That falls amid the shades of gloom,
Her gentle presence softly threw
    A suasion round, that called in bloom
The buds of every manly part
That hidden lies within his heart.
He reared his home in better style,
    He robed himself in better taste,
His boisterous laugh became a smile,
    Frugality succeeded waste;
He made the desert as a rose
    To bloom along her gentle way;
The world around was all repose
    Beneath her kind, her loving sway;

Like oil upon the troubled sea,
   She calmed the current of his mind ;
She bid his stormy passions flee,
   And gave us social man refined.

Then came those days of great unrest,
When all the world seemed moving West ;
When there, a stream of people run
Like Pilgrims to the setting sun :
And as this road was of its class
The best across the mountain-pass,
Here poured that ever-ceaseless tide,
That drained the country far and wide,
And bore, or so it seemed, a trace,
Of every clime and every race,
   A headlong, heedless swarm.
Old age came tottering on his staff ;
The youth would pass with merry laugh ;
The jaded mother, and her child,
Went dragging on toward the wild ;

A frail, too oft, and helpless band,
To break a wild, unsettled land
And brave privation's storm.

But as the current onward rolled,
Some, like the patriarchs of old,
Moved flocks and herds, and well prepared
They bore their tents, the herdsmen shared;
And seemed, indeed, but to repeat
In substance Abram's life complete.

Then, too, the heavy teams would pass,
The symbols of another class;
Hale farmers, solid men of worth,
Whose skilful hands control the earth,—
 Their wagons, on the road,
Were all broad-wheeled, and iron-bound,
Less prone to cut the swarded ground;
 And built to bear a load.
Their shapes were mostly curved below,
Much like an upturned flattened bow;

While overhead were arches bent
And roofed with canvas like a tent,
To shield the old,—to house the young,
Who still around the mother clung;
While by their side, along the road,
The farmer trudged, or driving strode
A wheel-horse, chosen from a breed
Of strength, peculiar, for his need.

And then would come the humble cart,
That served a poor, ambitious heart,
Whose wife and babe perched up before,
The sum of all his earthly store,
Went with him, toiling on, to find
The Eldorado of his mind.

And in the stream the pack-mule passed,
A het'rogeneous pile amassed;—
A grand display of human skill
Which made the means at hand fulfil

THE RETROSPECT.

Their dire need ; and with surprise,
I've watched them oft with puzzled eyes,
To see how such a varied load
Could keep together on the road.
The loads were mixed, of bedding, tools,
And grindstones, packed upon the mules;
With axes, scythes, and earthenware,
And stoves, and tins, for household care;
The food the owner most would need
Along the road, and bags of seed,
All lashed around so close and tight
The beast was scarcely left in sight.

And then, the ox-team's movements slow
Was ever in that ceaseless flow;
While falling still behind the throng
It dragged its measured pace along,—
A gait so sluggish none could stand,
Except it moved towards a land
O'er which Hope cast that phantom beam
That dazzles every dreamer's dream.

But when at last the sun for rest
Rolled down the confines of the west,
Then for the night a halt was made,
On mountain, road, or in the glade,
As chanced the trav'llers, there they stayed
   And lit their evening fire:
Where all the labors round were shared;—
The mother and the young prepared
The evening meal; while men with care
Groomed all their horses, spread their fare,
   And did what might require
Such things as needed strength of frame;
As hewing wood to feed their flame,
   Which burned the night entire.
For every camp a watcher's blaze
Kept for its night-protecting rays;
While all the wayworn sought their sleep
   In wagons round—on nature's breast,—
Save those who did the vigil keep:—
   Then onward for the West!

THE RETROSPECT. 79

Yes, sought their rest,—a precious prize
  To honest toilers of the clod!
Who turn to God their hopeful eyes,
  Though resting on their native sod!
But what a place!—a dreary blight!
  Are beds of down when revel's brain
Seeks for repose, as fades the night
  That marks a soul with sorrow's stain.
Sleep comes not when the conscience burns
  The brand of doom upon the heart,
Nor silken shades, nor scented urns,
  Can bid the evil haunt depart.
But to the man whose life is spent
  In worthy deeds of good intent,
There comes within his honest breast
  A calm, that gives a peaceful rest.
Rest for the weary!—what a sound!—
  It seems an echo from the sky,
While guardian angels wait around,
  To guide a fleeting soul on high.

But as I've called in quick review
Those passing groups, like pictures new,
I gave but scenes when skies were fair,
Withholding those of dark despair
That daily came before the eye,
Among the hapless passers-by.
But time has never once effaced
A single scene that anguish traced
Upon my heart when forced to stay,
Beholding wrecks along the way,—
    Like one who from her sea-girt home
Appalling!—sees, beneath the frown
Of storming clouds, a bark go down;—
All helpless, while the hopeless drown
    Amid the seething foam!

CANTO III.

The moon, round as an ancient shield,
Full, argent burnished, held the field
    Against the hosts of night.
Eclipsed were all,—save but a few
Bright, glowing stars, that kept in view
    The glory of their light.
But of the group—none marked the time,—
None marked the glowing scene sublime—
All listened to the tales as told
Of their determined kindred old,
Who, with their brave compatriots bold,
Had settled first this trackless wold,
    In days long passed away:
And list'ning looked, in reverent awe,
On her who all those changes saw,
    As she resumed the lay.

While in the West the mingling throng
Implanted firm an empire strong;
Its days, at first, saw thousands there
Arrive to perish in despair:
For few indeed, who felt the hand
   Of poverty, could find again
The means, or strength, to reach the land
   They left, to swell the westward train;
For through the country, scattered wide,
The onward, outward, selfish tide
Had calmly learned to coldly see
Privations in their worst degree.

I well remember, now, the time,
'Twas in the Summer's middle prime,
   A drought, when days were warm,
Had lingered long, when looming high
Along the margin of the sky
All things appeared; forewarning nigh
   A coming eastern storm.

It was indeed a busy day ;
The farmers strove to guard the hay,
To stack the grain, and well prepare
Against the threatened winds with care.
At last,—toward the evening hour,
Plutonic-black, began to lower
Both east and west with swelling storms,
Which rolling came like mountain forms
Arrayed to meet,—and filled with woe
All living things on earth below.
The wild beasts for a refuge fled ;
The cattle hurried home in dread ;
While men who had the taste and time
Beheld a scene at once sublime.
The massive clouds approaching rolled
Wild as the flocks that left the fold,
Impelled by some appalling fright,—
Or like the eagles in their flight,
The ragged racks careered on high ;
Until they deeply veiled the sky.

Then for a moment nature stood,
   As armies, breathless, ere the strife
Arouses up the fiend of blood,
   To revel in the waste of life.
No breath of air,—the very leaf
Stood motionless, a moment brief,
When 'thwart the dome the lightning flashed ;—
The simultaneous thunders crashed ;
While circling gusts came sweeping by
That twirled the dust and leaves on high,
Until the big descending rain
Drove all things back to earth again.

The lightnings flashed ; the thunders roared
Continuous, while the showers poured ;
As if indeed old Jove, in might,
Was storming every mountain-height ;
Or Noah's days had come again,
A deluge in the falling rain ;
And this terrific scene of awe,
Surpassing all I ever saw,

Continued in its might and power
Until the night's deep middle hour.

'Twas on that wild, tempestuous night
Two women, with a babe, in fright,
Within our barn a refuge sought,
All drenched,—for they were tempest caught;
   And near appeared their end.
Dark was their gloom, and deep their care,—
The storm,—their want,—their blank despair :
And death-like sickness, too, was there,
   And they without a friend.
But He who hears the raven's cry
Neglected not the prayerful sigh,
   But proved a friend indeed.
For Reuben, from his steady course,
Was moved by some resistless force
   To serve their pressing need.
Impelled, or by an impulse led,
He rose and left his midnight bed

To go and see if aught befell
The cattle housed,—if all were well.
For sleep had fled,—he could not stay
Until the coming dawn of day.

As Reuben went, on drawing nigh,
He heard a baby's sickly cry
Come from the barn;—and then a song,
The words were mixed with sobs along
The lines, that bore a strange refrain;
Attuned to some pathetic strain.
It seemed to cease,—and then a cry,—
And then the mother's sob, and sigh,
All blending in this lullaby:

Hush, my baby! though the thunder
Tore the storming clouds asunder,
Pouring down their deluge under,
  God the Father ruled the sky.
   Hush, my baby! hush, my baby!
  God is love, and ever nigh.

THE RETROSPECT. 87

Stars, while clouds above were weeping,
Still were shining,—never sleeping,—
Hovering angels watch were keeping,
    While the tempest rent the air.
        Hush, my baby! hush, my baby!
    Angels watched my darling fair.

Dews of evening feed the flowers;
Growing harvests drink the showers;
Little baby's brightest hours
    Come in love's own peaceful rest,
        Hush, my baby! hush, my baby!
    Sleeping on its mother's breast.

Little bees will gather honey
When the days are bright and sunny,
Baby's boon, unbought for money,
    Is its sleep without a fear:
        Hush, my baby! hush, my baby!
    Is its sleep with Jesus near.

Daily hours have told their number;
Butterflies in roses slumber;
Nothing should thy dreams encumber;
   Blessful dreams from realms above.
      Hush, my baby! hush, my baby!
   Lord of mercy guard my love!

When Reuben paused to learn the why
Of all those sobs,—that sickly cry,—
He heard, while moving round with care,
Behind the mow, a stifled prayer
Come from a woman pleading wild,
That God would save a dying child.

It was a breaking heart that poured
Her plea to Him her soul adored,
   As few have ever prayed:
For with the child she craved for one
   The hand of mercy's tender care;
For one,—the widow of her son,
   So true,—so young,—so fair.

So true,—whose steps had been delayed
By filial love's unselfish arm
That strove to shield, from every harm,
Her tottering age through dread's alarm;
And then again her prayer grew wild,—
"Oh, let me perish!—Save the child!"

Then back, with quick impatient speed,
Came Reuben from that place of need;
Came bidding me arise! for Death
Was waiting for a lingering breath!
While one was sending prayers on high
That she might for another die!

But then an anxious care arose
Between us, how we might disclose
The fact that coming aid was near,
Lest we might terror add to fear.
I bid him sing,—I knew that voice
Could make despair itself rejoice.

THE RETROSPECT.

I knew it, well!—its force was clear,
As sounds the trumpet through the air
When cheering on in martial might
His braves, recoiling in the fight,—
Or soft in peace, as sighs the flute;
Or gentle as the lover's lute;
When friendship, or when mercy's call
Had roused a heart that throbbed for all.

Then rich in cadence, softly clear,
He raised a grand, sweet, sacred air;
Which rolled like swelling notes that bore
God's promise to a shipwreck shore.
I never heard him sing again
   So like an angel, as it rung
Clear, yet subdued, that blest refrain
   When thus my noble Reuben sung:

Oh! bear to the Saviour your burden of sorrow,
   His all-searching eye is beholding your grief;

Though night's sable shadows are dark, yet the morrow
 Is sure by His promise to bring its relief.

Though wild beat the tempest,—though wild winds were blowing,
 The Lord o'er His children was watching below;
And from the free fountains of grace, overflowing,
 He sends the rich blessings His mercies bestow.

Beyond the world's darkness forever is shining
 That Light o'er the billows of sorrow and gloom;
Where love, and where faith, and where grace, all combining,
 Will guide to their glory the blest of the tomb.

Then trust to the Master each heart of affliction,
 The Lord calls His own beloved children to come;
And He will reward with that blest benediction,
 That fits us to dwell in His glorified home.

While time shall last, I'll ne'er forget
  The scene, within the barn, we saw,
On entering there,—I see it yet!
  The woman!—babe!—the scattered straw!
Recalled to me in majesty
My dream of the nativity.
A woman young, of queenly grace,
Was on her knees,—her hallow'd face
Was all aglow,—her soft blue eyes
Were raised, to supplicate the skies.
Love swayed the soul;—it was not fear
Which brought the gush,—the sparkling tear,
That fell upon her faded child;—
I saw it turned but once, and smiled,
As first, amid the gloom of night,
It caught our lantern's sudden light;
Then fainted on its mother's breast,
Like one in death's eternal rest.

And then the agéd saint was there,
Relieved, and strengthened,—for her prayer

Had brought a peace unknown to those
Who stand as God's rebellious foes.
Calm was her brow, her spirit won
    Faith's resignation from on high;
Calm as when storms their course have run
    And left to peace a cloudless sky,
Where glory's hosts triumphant shine,
With all their radiant lights divine.

Yet haggard was her face,—it bore
Deep marks of dread privation sore;
While with a modesty refined
She still displayed her cultured mind,
In striving to excuse, with grace,
Their storm-forced trespass in the place.
But with a word,—a kindly word,
We checked her story—half unheard;
And bid them move with instant speed,—
For we had learned their helpless need
And both in urgent haste had come,
With help, with comfort, and a home.

Oh! such a scene!—when grief, repressed,
Is turned to joy in sorrow's breast,
   I never saw before.
The wringing hands,—the gushing eyes,
The stifled words,—the broken cries,—
Gave thankful tokens of surprise
   At mercy's gifts in store.

And when toward the babe we turned,
Aglow my heart with pity burned;
For Death, to all appearance there,
   Had marked that tiny bud to deck
   His march of ruin o'er the wreck,
Where buried lay the old and fair,
Beneath the ploughman's thoughtless share.

But care, and watchfulness, and prayer,
   All night in earnest, constant strife,
Did much ere morning to repair
   That flick'ring flame of life.

For with the dawn the lengthened breath
Proclaimed our triumph over Death,
And health returning gave again
The child to soothe the mother's pain.

But she who kindly, grandly gave
Her life, a sacrifice to save
The little babe, we quickly saw
   Had been accepted in its stead ;
An offering free, to fill the law
   That gives to Death his numbered dead,—
Yes, passed away—to realms of peace
Where cares, and tears, and sorrows cease,—
Yes, called to furl—her time was o'er—
Life's tattered sails on Jordan's shore,
To find above, at Glory's shrine,
The saint's eternal rest divine.

FAITH was her name,—and of that stock
Who followed those of Plymouth rock ;

Strong, earnest men, a sturdy race
Who every danger dared to face
  That crossed their honest path :
Be it a wrong to freedom's right;
An ill that might their conscience blight;
Or war's wild raging, when the fight
  Terrific rolls in wrath.
But she was gentle as a dove,
Calm in her faith, strong in her love;
And ever ready stood to share
With others all their toiling care.

And strangely checkered was her life,
Its joys were few, and much its strife ;—
Her maidenhood, of happy years,
Were spent without affliction's tears.
But scarcely had she reached that hour
When youthful bliss, beneath the bower
Of nuptial love,—in love reclining,—
Building castles,—all divining,—
  Deemed earth's cares were o'er,

THE RETROSPECT.

When o'er New England widely spread
The Revolution's cloud of dread,
  That told of coming war.
I've heard her tell, how on the night
Preceding Bunker Hill's fierce fight,
She heard the constant, steady tramp,
Of soldiers marching to the camp,—
For Charlestown was her home, and there
  The yeomanry of Freedom came,
In all their conscious power, to dare
  Great Britain's bands of martial fame:
And first in Freedom's host to go
Her husband sped, to meet the foe;—
Sped on that night, and left alone
His youthful wife and babe at home.

That night, in terror's deep dismay,
She waited, weary, for the ray
Of morning; when, behold, around
The hills were seen with ramparts crowned;
  A challenge to the foe.

A challenge to the royal host,
Who launched, to charge the rebel coast,
   And lay rebellion low.
She saw them land and charge the hill;
   She saw them storm the strong redoubt;
She saw the might of Freedom's will
   When Death's wild flash rolled fiercely out,
And mowed the soldiers of the crown,
As reapers sweep the harvest down.
Recoiling back,—they charged again,
Like wild waves from the angry main;
Then back, again in terror bore,
As breakers from a rock-bound shore:
Again,—till legions fell again,
That tyrants might a land enchain.

The while, firm anchored on the tide,
Lay England's royal oaks of pride,
   Like monsters of the deep.
Aroused,—their guns all charged with shell,
They opened ports,—when fires of hell

Blazed from their sides against the shore;—
Their thunders swelled with awful roar;
While Charlestown, all to sate their ire,
From hearth to roof, was wrapt in fire
　　That skyward strove to leap.
She saw her home in embers smoke;
She found her husband,—but he spoke
No more to her;—by Warren's side
He bravely fought, and nobly died.

There was her home in ashes spread.
Flown was her hope,—her husband dead:—
Her all on earth were gone,—save one
Poor tiny thing, a helpless son—
A helpless child, where all could trace
The impress of its father's face,
Alone, was left by fate, to throw
A blessing o'er her path of woe.
Her tale was one so often told,
It seemed a theme of sorrows old,

A toiling widow—sighs and tears—
An anxious mother's hopes and fears—
Her doubt of every thoughtful plan,
Until her boy became a man.

Then bright again her star arose,
  To herald in a hopeful day,
With every promise of repose,
  With filial love's resplendent ray.
Such love as cheers the mother's heart,
As blunts the point of sorrow's dart,
As smooths the rugged round of life
In all its ceaseless whirl of strife.
E'en in his choice, a fortune rare
Came with his bride, a Christian fair;
A guide, a stay, a gem was she,
Of every selfish impulse free;
A wife to him, a daughter blest
  To Faith's old age;—like Ruth sublime
She gave her arm,—a stay of rest,
  Supporting down the paths of time

The mother of that one, above,
Whose mem'ry bound their deathless love.
So bound as one,—their home was strong;
Love there reposed without a wrong;
  No jealousy, no jarring strife:
No poison-fang to mar or blight,—
They knew naught but the path of right;
  The mother, son, and wife.
But then that season of unrest
Illumed their fancy for the West,—
For they believed in faith, as true,
The phantasies that Fortune drew;
And swelled the tide, that rolled away,
Along the onward course of day.

They found, indeed, the forest grand !—
But then that wild, unbroken land
Required the firm, the steady hand
  Of might, to break the virgin sod;
While all their strength was that of mind,
Their statures all were light, refined,
  Ill suited to the clod.

But with undaunted courage true
  The father built their forest home;
With comforts equalled there by few,
  And bravely broke the stubborn loam ;
When fell Disease, with blighting breath,
Came as the messenger of Death,—
Came with his deep, dark, sullen frown,
And struck the man with fever down.

I've heard their story, o'er and o'er,
  How many an anxious,—trembling hour
They watched ;—and how the patient bore
  The fever's raging,—wasting power :
And how he firmly clung to life,
With hope, to shield his babe and wife,
And mother, where a savage race
Disputed every right of place.

I've heard them tell, how, when the hand
  Of Death he felt,—with dauntless nerve,

He bid them sell their stock and land ;—
And told which horse they should reserve
To draw them back whence they had come,
To build among their friends a home.
I've heard them tell, how dark the day,
When in his narrow couch of clay,
    They laid the father down ;
And how they both in anguish turned
Heart-broken from the home he earned,
    To meet misfortune's frown.

Their steed, howe'er, surpassed by few,
For step, for strength, for kindness true,
Gave both, with each succeeding day,
New confidence along the way ;—
Until at last, before their gaze
They saw the lofty mountains raise
    Like bulwarks to the very sky ;
Where Giants might their revels keep
On every castellated steep,
    Appalling to the eye.

I knew, myself, their road,—so grand!
Just as it was when nature's hand
　　Had rent the rocks in twain!
Or had, perhaps, in better mood,
The hardship of the way subdued,
　　Down to a level plain.
I've gone with Reuben often o'er
Their very road, in days of yore,
Before the vandal hand of man,
With many an engineering plan,
　　Despoiled rich beauty's store.

Description never can enhance
Those scenes in fact, or in romance.
Terrific! wild! the valleys deep
Would terrify—or from a steep
Grand landscapes, that all words defy,
Burst forth on man's enraptured eye;
　　Remembered evermore!
Oft would the road, through some wild glen,
Wind round a fern-bound mossy fen,

Or lead, where naught but slippery clay,
From leaping cascades' scattered spray,
Became, through gorges darkly deep,
But doubtful footing, hard to keep;—
And then, again, would slowly climb
To those broad scenes, so rich, sublime!
 Of which I spoke before.

These anxious women, with their child,
 By toiling on, had nearly gained
The boundary stream, that does divide
 The rugged from the rolling side,
  Before the close of day.
 For from the peak, that last remained,
They saw the winding river run,
 Just like a golden thread that drained
Its color from the setting sun :—
But long they found the road, that lay
In zigzags down the mountain way,
Consumed the fleeting time before
They forded to the distant shore,
 Beneath the twilight's ray.

And yet, though worn, with eager chase
They forward press'd, to reach the place
  Of some encamping outward train;—
For as they crossed the ford they found
Two footpads on the rising ground,
  That thrilled with terror every vein.
The scoundrels begged,—but all could see
Some deep design beneath their plea;—
  When startled by the rapid tread
Of horsemen, both the villains fled,
As if they, too, would cross by flight
The ford, before the fall of night.

But fear possessed each woman's thought:
Protection's hand was what they sought,—
On! on they pushed! but all in vain;
They found encamped no coming train;
And forced at last, in sheer dismay,
Strove hard to hide themselves away.
Deep, there, within a gorge they drove,
  Where trees, and vines, and chaparral,

Commingling formed a darksome grove,
   Like those where wolves and panthers dwell;
But sooner would they trust the den
Of preying beasts than prowling men.

Poor souls!—that night,—terrific night!
Hid,—crouching,—trembling,—all afright,—
They waited for the morning light
   In terror's depths of gloom.
Nor were they wrong;—at last they heard
The sound of voices,—sounds they feared,
   Pronounce their coming doom.
They heard vile disappointment's oath;—
They heard the counter-plans of both;—
As they were forced, with stifled breath,
To hear the villains argue death.
One argued murder;—for, he said,
Naught keeps a secret like the blade;
And that their every plan might fail
If one was left to tell the tale.

The other strove against the knife,
  And held it but a craven shame
To take a helpless woman's life,
  When plunder was alone the game.
That rob they could, and travel on,
Afar in safety ere the dawn,—
Just then their restless horse revealed
The place where all had been concealed;
And brought the robbers on their prey,
While turning from the search away.

I've seen these women deathly pale,
Rehearsing o'er their frightful tale;
Of how the would-be-murderer swore,—
How hope seemed gone for evermore;
When fiercely with his purpose set,
The fiend, to carry out his threat,
  Rushed forth to strike the blow.
And how his comrade, moved aright,
With what appeared a giant's might,

THE RETROSPECT. 109

Hurled back, in boisterous fury wild,
The worthless dastard, like a child,
   Among the brambles low.
And how the craven came, in fear,
Back, cringing, like a punished cur,
To make his act a jest appear;
   With doubtful step, and slow.

Though left unhurt—yet robbed they were
Of all but life, and dark despair;—
   A babe and helpless women twain!—
Their tale would bring but tears to hear
Each day of hardship, hope, and fear;
Until that stormy night severe,
   When thunders, lightnings, rush of rain,
   Drove in their wild alarm
The three beneath our hand of care,
To find, when all seemed but despair,
   A covert free from harm.

The child grew well,—the fatal spark,
Of death, had reached another mark;
Had reached that heart who pleading gave
Herself a sacrifice, to save
The little life,—that he might be
A solace on the mother's knee,—
And well he proved, in after-years,
  A recompense most richly given,
To her whose love, through toil and tears,
  Had blest a soul that soared to heaven.

The failing grandma's forced delay
Forever checked their homeward way;—
  To meet each day's demand,
Brave Grace determined, while she stayed,
To try her skill and thrift at trade;
And though she came with many a tear,
The smiles of Fortune kept her here,
  An honor to the Land.

CANTO IV.

SWIFT rolled the time—the hour was late,
Yet still the ancient queen held state;
While round, her maids-of-honor fair
Had clustered near the royal chair
In loving mood—with tender care.
Nor marked they how the moments flew;
Who heeds the time when tales are new?
And these to them were stories true.
One held her hand, some found a seat,
Like Paul at great Gamaliel's feet,
While all, without art's skilful care,
Had formed a group beyond compare.

Then to her band this sovereign said:
"Time flies, and I have long delayed,—
So I will not the time employ
With tales about the growing boy,

And all you cousins here can tell,—
Can all from certain knowledge draw
The stories of his manhood well,—
Your grandsire—and my son-in-law!

His fame has spread from shore to shore,
Where mountains rise and oceans roar.
In Senate of the nation great,—
Executive of this grand State,—
A minister of high report
Where England's Crown holds royal court;—
And proudly all the people tell
How honestly he served them well.
In politics he stood supreme
For honest worth and noble mien
Among that class which, sad to say,
Seems destined soon to pass away.

I've oft rejoiced—I've often told
How much improved are things of old;

And yet it grieves me to behold
  Corruptions of the State.
For now we see the tricksters guide
The fate of all; and fraud decide
The people's will for selfish aim,—
And I have wept, to see the shame
  Of this our modern date:
To know how in the slums by night,
Where Satan's sulphurs dim the light,
Conspiracies against the right
Of every man are formed;—and men
Are chosen in perdition's den
Who cater to the every taste
Of plunder, wrong, and public wast‧.

Once, public deeds were done in view
With every honest feeling true,
When all the land assembled wide
From hill and dale, on every side,
  To hold a barbecue

Nor was that feast, now passed away,
Barbaric in its simple day;
But formed a pageant rich and gay,
   Where gathered old and young.
The rich, that they might still retain
Their vaunted scope,—and then the vain,
As sycophants, would toady round
To every group throughout the ground,
   Where pride and power clung.
The honest farmer came to see
The would-be-leaders of the free;
And youth, and beauty, rich and rare,
Would come to visit fashion's fair,
   In all their bright attire.
The ancient mother, matron, maid,
Would come to grace the public glade,
With men of every social shade,
   From youth to tot'ring sire.

Political—the public call
Proclaimed a festival for all;

Presided o'er by chosen men,
  Who ruled with autocratic power
Supreme in each sequestered glen,
  Supreme throughout their bower:
Supreme, amid primeval trees
Whose branches, hailing every breeze,
  Cast cooling shades below:
Where rustic tables, rough and strong,
Were braced between the trees along,
  Or built to form a row.

For days there, on a spit-like pole,
  Before a monster fire,
They roasted swine, and oxen whole,
  Each barbecued entire:
And all that pleasure could advance,—
Pavilions for the festive dance— .
The feast the coming throng would share—
The managers, with every care,
  Done as it might require.

THE RETROSPECT.

Then came the morn—to mem'ry dear,
And found the anxious land astir,—
For twenty miles or more around,
    Found every class,—found each abode,
Preparing for the festive ground,
    Or moving on the road.
Their wagons, carts, were brought in play ;—
Their equipage of rich display ;—
With crowds that footed all the way,—
And speedy horses, dashing gay,
    By daring riders strode.

Then hands were clasped, and greetings past,
    With heart throughout the ground ;
There would the proud forget their caste,
    And with the plain be found :
Until the vast assembly grew
As neighbors, firm in friendship true,
All seeming with one thought in view,
    To find the men of state.

And knots would gather in a crowd,
And call for favored men, aloud,
Who ready found a stump at hand
That served for each, a speaker's stand,
    E'en for the ruling great :
And easy were it then to tell,
As cheers rose high, and cheers rolled long,
In wild excitement from the throng,
    The man in favor well.

The speaking done, a jubilee
Like horn assembled all the free
To dinner, 'mid the wildest glee ;
Where youthful knights, with gallant care,
To win their laurels, served the fair
    Around the teeming board.
And in return, each girl would serve,
All merry, as he might deserve,
    The palate of her lord.
Then to the dance, the mazy dance,
    The fiddle and the piping fife,

Called through the afternoon's expanse
   The young and hale to active life,
While Cupid's arrows flew apace,
And filled with wounded hearts the place.

'Twas in those scenes—those scenes of joy,
   The people caught the sparks of light
Shed by your grandsire, then a boy,
   Or scarcely more, when first in flight
His soul sublime took wings and soared
To heights the weak and wise adored.
His eloquence,—no tongue can tell
His mighty power,—the magic spell
By which he swayed the human heart
And swept its cords through every part.
His burning words each soul's desire
Would thrill,—and fill the eye with fire;
Would blanch the cheek with dangers near;
Could ope the fount of sorrow's tear;
Or at his grand, majestic will
Bid every troubled heart be still.

And such the man,—and such the men,
The people made their leaders then;
But oh! Behold! in sorrow bow,
To see the party rulers now!
Machinery now rules the day!
Professing politicians sway!
Who, Arnold-like in shame and vice,
Would sell their country for a price!
God help the people if they stand
And yield to demagogues the land;
Who seek to ride upon the tide
Of discontent on every side;
Who strive to foment anger, strife,
Between the rich and poor in life,
While common sense will tell to all
We must together stand or fall.
God save the land! Lord, may it be
A land forever blest by Thee!
A land of every land the best!
A refuge for the world's oppressed!

I see another cloud appear
That fills my aged heart with fear!
It makes my cheek with sorrow burn;—
An ill that modest worth should spurn.
It is a blight would dim the rose
  That blooms on purity's fair cheek,
'Twould chill the love of home's repose,
  Exalt the vile and crush the weak.
In woman's sacred name it craves
  For her the ballot's sovereign might,
The game of deep designing knaves,
  Who clamor round for " woman's right."
What are her rights—to leave her home
Amid the vicious haunts to roam?
Can virtue pure remain and meet
With prostitutes in their retreat,
Like snow upon the filthy street,
  And hope to mend the time?
When men of strength can scarcely stand
Against the vile on every hand,
  Who glory in their crime.

Heroic oft is woman's strife,
　When sad her fate appears as given,
Contending for the bread of life,
　To feed her brood,—a gift of Heaven.
But if she leaves her sacred sphere
A land accursed should quake with fear,
To see the worst of evils near.
Shall Cleopatra's evil fame,—
Shall vile Aspasia's open shame,
　Blight Liberty's fair brow?
And spread their curse o'er every hearth,
Where sits a wife of moral worth,
　In peace and comfort now.
Almighty hope! forbid the crime!
Long may true mothers rule sublime,
By Christian home-love's guiding hand!—
The will that trains!—controls the land!—
We see in Moses, now, the plan,
Whom God ordained to mould the man!

But I must cease my gloomy wail,—
A plain old woman's simple tale

Was all at first I thought to trace,
And tell how time had changed the place,
But strange 'twill seem when strangers tread,
In coming years, among our dead,
To see a tomb inscribed—" Unknown,"
As one among our sacred own :
And as my days are nearly o'er,
   I'll tell you all just how it came,
A stranger's tomb that never bore
   A shadowy trace of home or name,—
The story runs in times of old ;
Among the early dates I told.

'Twas in the Winter,—blighting chill,
The bleak winds swept from every hill ;—
Came howling 'mid the branches bare ;—
Came whirling dead leaves through the air ;—
As men brought in the wood, with care,
To keep our hearth, of bliss, aglow
Through that portentous storm of snow ;

For well we knew the signs o'erhead,
When leaden clouds all overspread
The skies with nature's sullen frown,
The storm must soon come sweeping down;
And so it did! ere morning's hour,
With wild Siberia's driving power,
It came—and baffles now to tell,
In language, how all day it fell;
Until in drifts, and plains below,
The world lay buried deep in snow.

That gloomy day, its sombre light,
Was blending with the gathering night;
When in our servant rushed, to state,
'A crazy man was at the gate:
A wild-like—helpless—half-clad form,
That seemed nigh frozen by the storm.'
We sought the door, and standing saw
A figure strange, that filled with awe
My heart,—in all my checkered days
I never saw so wild a gaze!

There, weird indeed, the figure stood,
Like some wild spectre of the wood,
Clothed in a garb of scant array
Unfit to brave a winter's day.

His moccasins were thin and old;
His pants were worn at every fold;
And coatless was his shivering form
While round, to guard him from the storm,
He drew a blanket, thin and bare,
That stood as naught against the air.
Grotesque, upon his head a gear
He wore, of crape and raccoon fur,
Which ended with the striped tails,
That hung behind a brace of trails:
While round his neck, beneath his jaw,
He wrapped a heavy twist of straw;—
And then what added to the sight,
The man, with snow, was covered white.

Blue was his face,—the chill of death
Seemed breathing from his icy breath,

THE RETROSPECT.

That rose as vapor, and appeared
Like frost upon his frozen beard;—
That sight unpitied none could see,
'Twas suffering in its worst degree.
I now can see his features thin,
As Reuben strove to coax him in,
From out that wild and blinding storm,
To share a refuge safe and warm.

Wild was his look,—his vacant stare
Made up the picture of despair;
Yet while refusing every aid,
In wandering words, he kindly said,
' I have no time, by night or morn!—
My pilgrimage is onward!—on!
    I'll grasp the wind!—
    I'll safely bind!
The tempest with a string!
    And then all day
    I'll watch and pray,
And hear the angels sing!

Do you hear! do you hear!
How sweetly, and clear,
They warble around! they're ever near!'

And yet again!—again we tried,
To have him but that stormy night
Come in, and safely there abide
Until the morrow's dawning light,
And break with us our evening bread,
That stood upon the table spread.
He paused—then heaved a heavy sigh,
While something calmed his restless eye;—
Yet still he gave this strange reply:
'I'll catch the snow
The wild winds blow,
For meal to make my bread!
But who will make
The bread, and bake,
For my poor wife is dead!
Whoo! whoo! what a dirge!

Around her grave these wild winds surge!
But storms must cease at glory's verge!'

All seemed as useless,—every plea
Was wasted, to the last degree,
Upon the man, who failed to see
  Naught but his visions wild.
When smiling came behind, to scan,
And peeped, to see the 'stranger-man,'
  Your grandma, then a child.
Her tiny smile was like a ray,—
It drove his clouds of doubt away,
  The man at once was changed.
He came, and took the proffered chair,
He shared the table's waiting fare,
And spent within the evening there,
  In not the least estranged:
And freely talked,—though strangely wild,
  Yet lucid moments came;
When he appeared serenely mild,
  Then thus would often name

His wife; who ever seemed a part
Of every dream that filled his heart:

'I had a wife! I blest the hour
I took my Marg'ret, not a flower
That ever bloomed was half so bright
As she, my heart!—her eyes of light
Shone like that pure and fadeless guide
Which seamen watch across the tide,—
True as that star, which marks the pole,
Was Marg'ret's faith, that thrilled her soul.
But Glory's gracious courts above
Were wanting angels; and my love
They called to realms of bliss on high,
Amid the mansions of the sky;
    Where storms shall cease!
    Where all is peace!
But yet they left our callow dove,
Our own, one, precious pledge of love.

'But oh! when in the chilly grave
    They laid her form,—all pleasure fled!

For all that earth in transport gave
  To me, lay sleeping with the dead.
It was not death!—she could not die!
  I knew my darling only slept,
And o'er her grave, when none were nigh,
  I nightly prayed, and watched, and wept,
And at her head I raised a cross,—
  An empty cross!—I raised it there;
To mark the lonely mound of moss
  That covers her, my matchless fair.
An empty cross! no drooping head!
No symbol of a Lord that's dead!
No figure telling by its gloom
That Death, triumphant, rules the tomb!
An empty cross!—The risen Lord!—
It symbolizes life restored!
And tells!—oh, what a jubilee!
That Marg'ret lives, and waits for me!
For me!—upon that deathless shore
Where howling storms shall rage no more."

THE RETROSPECT.

While talking thus, he seemed to be
  But dwelling on those thoughts refined
That once possessed his spirit free,
  Before affliction touched his mind.
But starting wildly up, he said,
'My precious time I've long delayed
And I must go! must go! must go!
Let howling tempests drive the snow!
What care I for the things below!
No house shall shield my troubled head!
My child is lost! my wife is dead!
Oh, let the cold winds bitter blow!
I'll seek the lost, through wind and snow!
And I must go! must go! must go!

'They took me to my little child
When it but slept! and sweetly smiled!
And said the little darling died!
And it should lie by Marg'ret's side!
  They lied! they lied!
  It never died!

'Twas but asleep!—
Oh! I could weep
To tell how they refused delay!—
And how they tore my child-away!—
As I! its father! on this arm
Was hugging its pale form from harm!
But round its cold,—its icy form,
I wrapt my coat to keep it warm;
And now I wear no coat! no! no!
For it would feel this biting snow!
An angel came and told me so!—
Before the storm the angel came,
And called my darling lamb by name;
And did to me this truth unfold:
When I am warm the child is cold;
And I will go!
Through wind and snow!
Until I find my precious fair!
With sky-like eyes! and flaxen hair!
That Marg'ret, when she soared above,
Left with me here!—Her child of love!"

THE RETROSPECT.

And then he took a bundle small,
That held its little clothing all,
And spread them out, with tender care,
To see if all were in repair.
And as he viewed the poor display,
   And turned the pieces o'er,
The madman seemed to pass away;
   As oft from mem'ry's store,
Kind words would fall, amid the maze,
That gave a glimpse of better days.

'This dress, all stitched along the band,
Was made,' he said, 'by Marg'ret's hand.
Yes! oft when night around had flung
Its mantle dark, she sewed, and sung
With me, the songs of love and praise;
The sweet refrain of brighter days.
Oh, these were happy times!—they're flown!
And I am left, alone! alone!

'This little coat, all wrought so fine,
Our baby's coat!—'twas hers and mine!

Was made when she, so thin and pale,
Looked haggard.—Oh! with no avail
I strove my bursting grief to hide,
As I sat loving by her side.
She saw that I was nearly wild,
When stooping o'er she kissed the child;
And asked me, as she saintly smiled,
That I should read to her, anon,
The fourteenth chapter of Saint John.
The mansion doors were open wide,
And soon she found her Saviour's side;
 But I was left
  The honored lot,
 Of her bereft,
  To mark the spot
Where Marg'ret sleeps, until that day
When Christ shall come in grand array;
And earth shall melt like wax away.
But none are left to mark the breast
Of mother-earth where I shall rest;

No! none to place a single stone
Or cross where I must sleep alone.

' And oh, these shoes! so worn and old,
Recalls me now my child is cold!
Lost! lost! oh, lost! she waits for me,
While time is ebbing like the sea!
How oft these little shoes, to meet
Thy mother's love, have borne thy feet!—
Have brought to me a welcome sweet!
    And yet while blowing
    Clouds are snowing
I've halting, stopped! Oh, woe is me!
I'm coming now! I'll come to thee!'

But we against his going stood,—
We humored every changing mood
    In kindness, to delay
The man till Reuben could prepare
In town a safe asylum there,
    Soon as returned the day.

But with a madman's cunning art
He shrewdly played a sleeper's part;
Till he perceived his watcher slept,
Then softly from the kitchen crept,
And found the child and mother's home,—
Above the storm,—in Glory's dome,—
For when the sun rose, all aglow,
We tracked the stranger o'er the snow,
And found a frozen form below.

Poor Reuben, moved with pitying grief,
  Wept o'er a sight so sad to see,
Although it gave a soul relief,
  And set the wanderer's spirit free.
And all remaining yet to do
We did, with Christian feeling true.
We gave to this wild stranger's head
A resting-place among our dead,
And carved upon his cross of stone,
'To Marg'ret's spouse—a poor unknown.'

But I have wandered long, to tell
  The incidents and scenes I saw,
In changes that around me fell,
As moved by some strange occult spell,
  And not by nature's law.
But when I wandered on this range
  We left the place a thriving town,
And yet, it seems a power strange,
That made that village by its change
  This city of renown.

In vain I look around to find
A scene familiar to my mind,
As when the red man's warlike hand
Did battle for his native land:
But all in vain;—the grand array
Reveals the old has passed away;—
No!—not one poor old Indian brave
Remains to deck his father's grave,
Or tell how once his savage race
Were masters of this settled place.

An alien people well may dread
The bold Caucasian's onward tread;
If they but meet, or cross his frown,
The ruthless white man ploughs them down.

But to the country came a rest,
As thriving cities filled the West;—
 The commerce with the East
Conveniences for travel made,
And transportations for the trade,
 As things around increased.

Long wagon trains, the freighted class
Like merchant fleets, would daily pass;
And proudly on they bore their course,
With bells arched o'er each leading horse;
 Arched o'er their collars broad.
That gave a merry signal clear,
A jingling, chime-like, ringing air,
 To all upon the road:

And then, the stage, in bright array
Passed swiftly by, and dashed away ;—
His four-in-hand the driver held,
While every heart with rapture swelled,
Within, to look, to hear, and see
The people in their merry glee,
Who cheered them as they swept along,
Or gave an echo to their song.

And at the station all was life,
All bustle,—all in active strife;
Where hostlers dashed about with speed
To groom the panting, smoking steed
    That late so quickly flew :
Or harness for the onward trip ;—
To hear the driver crack his whip!
    Then quickly out of view !
But every gilded cloud we see
Has still a shadow on the lea,
    Where brightest flowers dwell.

And staging had its dismal side,
To those whom business forced to ride,
   That broke the fancy spell.
For with an uncongenial throng,
   Their time appeared a cruel waste,
All jostled, with a crowd along
   Devoid of courtesy or taste:
Where nothing could relieve the thrall
That bound them in a space so small.

And oft the driver's early horn
   Aroused the village by its blast,
To see a weary crowd, forlorn,
All dusted o'er, and travel-worn,
   With heads of drooping cast.
For staging, through a chilly night,
Will make the best a sorry sight,
   To hail the coming morn.

Give me the steam! The modern steam!
That as a swallow skims the stream

The train sweeps on, and, like the wind,
Leaves distance, as a waste behind.
Far better than the stage of old,—
The heated cars defy the cold;
And human skill has in the race
Annihilated time, and space.

The grand hotels of modern time
Were never reached in dreams sublime
   By us in days of yore.
Where now the costly carpets greet
The tramp of every comer's feet,
   We had the sanded floor.
The wayside inn, in days of old,
Was but a kind of social fold,
Where man and beast could stop, and feel
At home; or find a hasty meal,
As time allowed a lengthened stay,
Or business urged their onward way.

THE RETROSPECT.

No architectural pile arose
Their stately grandeur to impose
　With domes, and turrets high.
Our ancient inns were mostly low,
Built all for use, with little show,
And near the door would standing be
A pump, and trough, and bucket free.
　For every passer-by.
While overhead a swinging sign,
Of letters,—or some crude design,
　Would catch the trav'ler's eye;
And tell the tavern standing there
Was one of comfort,—rich of fare,—
Built for the rover's special care.

Within,—the kitchen gave a view,
Indorsing much, the sign as true;
For from the spacious hearth the blaze
Would send its heat, and cast its rays
Of gold, to gild away the gloom
Of every corner round the room.

And in the chimney-place there swung
An iron crane, and on it hung
The boiling vessels, in array,
That sung their merry roundelay;
While hanging from the rafters high
Were tongues, and hams, and flitch to dry;
    That gave a scene of cheer.
And round the hearth, in social chat,
Commingling, for the evening, sat
All those—the waiters of the inn,
And those who served the guests, within,
    From every scattered sphere.

Now gorgeous!—grand!—to grace our day—
Magnificent in rich display!
Hotels arise, that almost seem
The substance of an Eastern dream.
Each mirrored room,—Corinthian hall,—
Their crystal lights,—their comforts all,—
Where round, in winter, softly flows
A warmth that lulls us to repose,

As if the stately palace, grand,
Belonged to some enchanted land.
Not so the rural inns of old;
Rude were their drawing-rooms, and cold,
Naught but the log-piled hearth, whose heat,
Midway across the room, would meet
An arctic rigor from without,
That forced us in a group about
   The hearth, with blaze aglow;
Where merry hearts,—a buoyant throng!—
For people in those days were strong,
Would tell their tales, or pass the jest,
In rivalry, to prove the best ;—
   But this was long ago!

And yet, I often loath to praise
The change of time;—for pride displays
A falling off, we all can trace,
In what evolves a manly race.
The girl, who only dreams of roses,
As she on silk and down reposes,

Presents a sorry sight,
As one to make a man a wife,
When forced to stem the tide of life
Against misfortune's blight.
I think the race, in torrid clime,
Those gardens of free birth,
Where nature's rich, prolific soil
Gives all to man without his toil,
And leaves his life a dearth,
Would quickly reach their end of time,
Amid their gorgeous scenes, sublime,
If they were not repeopled there
With north-men, who in frozen air
Had fought their sterile hills, amain,
Their scanty needs of life to gain.
So boys, who reared as tender plants,
Are apt to prove but frail gallants;
Unfit to serve their country's need;
Unfit to do a daring deed;
Unfit to brave, in manly strife,
The struggles of an active life.

But I must stop!—
            And yet a thought
Has on my flying fancy caught!—
There is a mighty change, no breath
Can tell its wonders.—It is Death!
I've seen its work;—of all who trod
This land at first, above the sod
I!—only I! remain to-day;
The rest—the rest have passed away.
The change has brought strange men unknown,
To those who gathered with our own;
And as I o'er the scene survey,
I wonder, where, oh! where are they;
The many who have met their doom
Of fate beyond the silent tomb?

Death gathers all, of human mould,
Within his dark eternal fold.
The poor, the rich, the weak, the brave;
    The beggar's rags,—the king his crown;
    Both worthless,—both must lay them down,
And sleep within the grave.

O mystery of mysteries! Thou
To whom the living world must bow;—
Thou canst but conquer things of earth;
The righteous have a blessed birth;
From all the might that rests in thee,
When thou hast set the spirit free.
I've watched the hero's parting sigh
I've seen the honored statesman die;
I've laid the baby from my breast
Down in its narrow couch of rest;
But soon I wiped my tears away,
For well I knew a brighter day
They saw, where we shall meet above,
In Glory's dome of deathless love.

I go!—and you must follow soon,
Though now in vigor's youthful bloom;
For all must soon receive the call
That spreads for us the sable pall.
Oh, what is pride! oh, what is power!
Or pomp in that dread final hour!

When every form of mortal clay,
Must fade to dust, and pass away!
I've often wondered what we love
   In those of earth, to whom we cling?
But logic—science—fail to bring
A reason, or a fact, to prove
   The mystery of the thing.

We see around the couch of death
The loved ones watch the fleeting breath;—
The potions,—vying hands prepare,—
The couch is smoothed with tender care,—
They stand, and watch the taper light
Of life, that's flickering in their sight;
Until the spirit takes its flight:
Then turn, and leave to strangers' hands
To do the last the world commands;
And quickly bear away that form,
Which once with love and life was warm.

I know we love the soul!—and why?
Because the soul can never die!
If thou wouldst test this truth, go tell
The tender tale, and watch the spell;
'Tis from the eye we see the glow
Of love's soft beam so sweetly flow,
That for a moment sorrow's power
Is lost in Eden's blissful hour.
But when the spirit-soul has fled,
Go whisper to the silent dead;
And watch the eye,—the glassy stare
Will tell that love's no longer there.
O death! thy bitter sting has flown
When God but gathers in his own.
O grave! thy victory is o'er
When we shall meet on Canaan's shore.

But now, before we say good-night,
Just look above;—behold the sight,—
The starry hosts, without a rest,
Are ever sinking in the west;

While from the brink of eastern space
Roll others up to fill their place :
And in the dome of spangled light
There shines the brilliant queen of night,
Who pours around her silv'ry beam,
Like floods of blessing, all serene.
And so mankind, since time had birth,
Has sunk from off the living earth ;
While others rise, to fill the room
Of those who pass to meet their doom.
Yet over all, oh, glorious sight!
The spirit sees Jehovah's light,
Who came, incarnate, here to save
The lost, from dark perdition's grave.
Light-of-the-world, Almighty ray,—
Incarnate God ! oh, guide our way !
Until at last, by mercy's grace,
We all shall see Thy hallow'd face !

Good-night! good-night!—before in sleep
   We close our eyes,—in earnest prayer,

We'll pray our Father God to keep
  Us all within His special care.
Good-night!—for good it is to be
From sickness, pain, and sorrow free;
To dwell in peace, without a fear,
In kindred love's own circle dear.

Good-night! remember, ere we sleep,
  The thoughtless sinner ever nigh;
The heathen dark,—the poor who weep,
  And crave them mercies from on high.
And then, return for blessings given,
Our own best heartfelt thanks to Heaven;
That we, in these our fleeting years,
Are placed beyond the gloom of tears.

Good-night! good-night! I give you here
  Such blessings as my love can give;
And oh, my children, ever dear!
  I pray that you in God may live.

That you may walk the path of right,
Nor ever wander from His sight;
That He will guide us by His might,
Until we sleep in death, good-night.
Good-night! good-night! good-night! good-night!"

THE END.

www.ingramcontent.com/pod-product-compliance
Lightning Source LLC
Chambersburg PA
CBHW031459160426
43195CB00010BB/1031